The 20 Unbreakable Rules of Personal Finance

Master Your Money, Master Your Life: The Ultimate Guide to Financial Freedom

Ashish Singh

© 2024 Ashish Singh

All rights reserved. No part of this book may be reproduced or transmitted in any form or by any electronic or mechanical means, including photocopying, recording, or by any information storage and retrieval system, without the prior written permission of the author, except where permitted by law.

This book is a work of dedication and passion, crafted to provide valuable insights and strategies for aspiring entrepreneurs and business leaders. The content herein has been developed by the author, Ashish Singh, drawing from a wealth of knowledge, experience, and the guidance of advanced AI tools such as Claude and OpenAI. These tools have assisted in refining the ideas and ensuring the accuracy of the information presented, enhancing the overall quality of this work.

Published by Ashish Singh

First Edition

Acknowledgements

This book, while bearing my name, is the result of countless contributions, both direct and indirect. It stands on the shoulders of giants in the field of personal finance and draws inspiration from the innovative approach of Al Ries and Jack Trout's "The 22 Immutable Laws of Marketing."

First and foremost, I want to express my deepest gratitude to the financial pioneers whose work has shaped the landscape of personal finance. Warren Buffett, Jack Bogle, Robert Kiyosaki, Dave Ramsey, and many others - your insights and principles have been invaluable in formulating these rules.

To my family, especially Sweta, your unwavering support and patience during the long hours of writing and research have been the bedrock upon which this book was built. Your belief in me and this project has been a constant source of motivation.

To my colleagues and mentors in the financial industry, your discussions, debates, and shared experiences have contributed immeasurably to the depth and breadth of insights in this book.

To the countless individuals who have shared their financial journeys with me - your stories of triumphs and struggles have given life to these principles and reminded me of the real-world impact of financial decisions.

Finally, to you, the reader. Your desire to take control of your financial future is what gives this book its purpose. Thank you for trusting me to guide you on this journey.

Remember, these rules are unbreakable, but it's up to you to apply them. Here's to your financial success.

Table of Contents

Preface
Introduction
Rule 1: The Compound Effect
Rule 2: The Lifestyle Deflation Doctrine
Rule 3: The Cushion Commandment
Rule 4: The Diversification Decree
Rule 5: The Autopilot Advantage
Rule 6: The Knowledge Leverage Law
Rule 7: The Debt Destroyer Directive
Rule 8: The Gratification Postponement Principle
Rule 9: The Multiple Streams Mandate
Rule 10: The Tax Tactician's Triumph
Rule 11: The Target Acquisition Theory
Rule 12: The Asset Allocation Axiom
Rule 13: The Frugal Innovation Formula
Rule 14: The Brutal Honesty Benchmark
Rule 15: The Perpetual Pivot Protocol
Rule 16: The Protection Paramount Principle
Rule 17: The Generosity Growth Gambit
Rule 18: The Opportunity Cost Calculus
Rule 19: The Decade Domination Doctrine
Rule 20: The Freedom Formula
Epilogue
Appendix
References

Preface

Money. It's been called the root of all evil, the measure of success, the source of happiness, and the cause of misery. But in reality, money is simply a tool - perhaps the most powerful tool in modern society. And like any tool, its impact depends entirely on how you use it.

This book isn't about getting rich quick. It's not about finding loopholes in the tax code or discovering the next hot stock. It's about something far more valuable: mastering the fundamental rules of personal finance.

In the following pages, you'll discover 20 Unbreakable Rules that govern financial success. These aren't tips or suggestions. They are laws as immutable as gravity, as constant as the speed of light. Violate them at your own risk.

Some of these rules will challenge your preconceptions about money. Others will seem obvious once stated, yet you'll realize you've been breaking them your entire life. All of them, if followed, will dramatically alter your financial trajectory.

From the nearly miraculous power of compound interest to the crucial importance of financial honesty, from the unexpected benefits of strategic generosity to the true meaning of financial freedom - these rules cover the entire spectrum of personal finance.

Each rule is presented with uncompromising clarity, illustrated with real-world examples, and concluded with a prediction of how violating it will impact your future in our rapidly evolving world.

This book will make you uncomfortable. It will challenge your habits, your beliefs, and possibly even your identity. Good. Comfort is the enemy of growth, especially when it comes to finance.

But if you have the courage to internalize and apply these 20 Unbreakable Rules, you'll find yourself on a path to financial success that no market crash, no technological disruption, no global crisis can derail.

The choice is yours. You can continue to stumble through your financial life, breaking rules you didn't even know existed. Or you can master these laws and use them to craft a future of prosperity and freedom.

Turn the page. Your financial revolution begins now.

Introduction

The Financial Revolution in Your Hands

In the world of personal finance, as in physics, there are fundamental laws that govern success and failure. Ignore them at your peril.

This book will not teach you how to get rich quick. It won't reveal a secret stock pick that will make you a millionaire overnight. If that's what you're looking for, put this book down now and go buy a lottery ticket. Your odds are about the same.

What this book will do is far more valuable. It will give you the 20 Unbreakable Rules of Personal Finance - principles that, if followed, will inevitably lead to financial success. These aren't tips or suggestions. They are iron laws, as immutable as gravity.

Some of these rules will challenge what you think you know about money. Good. Your preconceptions about finance are likely what's holding you back. Others will seem obvious once stated, yet you'll realize you've been violating them your entire life. Best to stop that now.

From the power of compound interest to the necessity of brutal financial honesty, from the surprising growth that comes from strategic generosity to the freedom that true wealth provides - these rules cover the entire spectrum of personal finance.

Each rule is presented with stark clarity, backed by real-world examples, and concluded with a prediction of how violating it will impact your future in our rapidly changing world. These predictions aren't wild guesses, but logical extrapolations of current trends. Ignore them at your own risk.

This book isn't for the faint of heart. It will challenge you. It will make you uncomfortable. It might even make you angry. Good. Comfort is the enemy of financial growth.

But if you have the courage to internalize and apply these 20 Unbreakable Rules, you'll find yourself on a path to financial success that no market crash, no technological disruption, no global crisis can derail.

The financial revolution is in your hands. Turn the page, and let it begin.

Rule 1: The Compound Effect

Small actions, repeated consistently, yield exponential results

In 1626, Native Americans sold Manhattan for $24 worth of beads and trinkets. A bad deal? Not if they'd invested it at 8% interest. Today, that $24 would be worth over $60 trillion - more than enough to buy Manhattan back, and then some.

This is the Compound Effect in action. It's not just a financial principle; it's a law of nature.

The Compound Effect states: Small, consistent actions, given enough time, will always outperform large, inconsistent efforts.

This rule applies whether you're earning minimum wage or pulling in seven figures. A janitor who invests $100 a month for 40 years will end up wealthier than a doctor who waits until 45 to start saving $1,000 a month.

The power of compound interest is why Warren Buffett made 99% of his wealth after his 50th birthday. It's also why credit card companies are some of the most profitable businesses in the world.

Ignoring this rule is financial suicide. Every day you delay is costing you future wealth. That $5 coffee isn't just $5 - it's $50 you won't have in retirement.

Compound interest is the financial equivalent of a snowball rolling downhill, growing larger with each revolution. It's returns on returns, profits on profits.

Many believe that saving more is the key to wealth. They're wrong. Time is the key, and compound interest is the lock.

Consider Vanguard, the investment giant. Founded in 1975, it took 25 years to reach $500 billion in assets. In the next 17 years, it hit $5 trillion. That's the power of compound growth.

Still not convinced? Let's look at two investors: Mike and Bob. At 20, Mike invests $2,000 annually at 7% return. Bob waits until 30, then invests double - $4,000 annually at the same rate. By 60, Mike has $428,000, Bob only $375,000. Mike invested $80,000, Bob $120,000. Yet Mike is $53,000 richer.

This isn't financial sorcery. It's the Rule of Compound Interest at work.

"But I'm already 30 (or 40, or 50)!" you might say. Remember: The best time to plant a tree was 20 years ago. The second-best time is now. Compound interest doesn't care when you start, only that you do.

Fidelity Investments found that 88% of their 401(k) millionaires built their wealth gradually over time, not through sudden windfalls or high salaries. They understood and harnessed the Rule of Compound Interest.

Many dismiss compound interest because the effects aren't

immediately visible. It's like watching grass grow - painfully slow at first. But given enough time, that same grass becomes a lush meadow.

The Rule of Compound Interest is unforgiving. It rewards the patient and punishes the procrastinator. No amount of financial acrobatics can make up for lost time.

The Compound Effect interacts powerfully with other rules in this book. It amplifies the benefits of The Lifestyle Deflation Doctrine (Rule 2) and is supercharged by The Autopilot Advantage (Rule 5).

Remember: In finance, as in life, consistency trumps intensity. Start small but start now. Your future self will thank you - or curse you - based on how well you heed this rule today.

Prediction: By 2050, AI-driven financial systems will automatically optimize every financial decision for compound growth. Those who don't understand and apply this rule will find themselves hopelessly behind, wondering why their high salaries never translated into real wealth.

Rule 2: The Lifestyle Deflation Doctrine

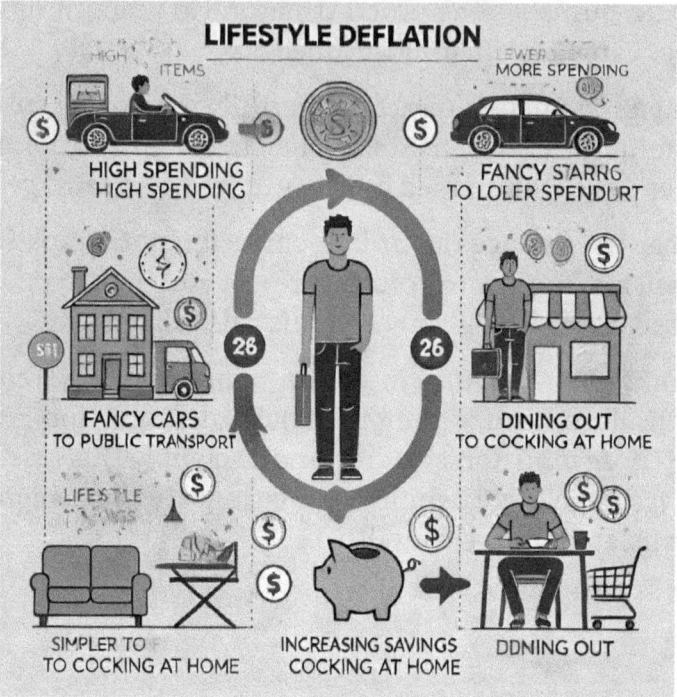

Spend less as you earn more, and watch your wealth explode

In 2009, NFL star Warren Sapp filed for bankruptcy. Despite earning over $40 million in his career, he found himself $6.7 million in debt. His crime? Lifestyle inflation.

The Lifestyle Deflation Doctrine is the antidote to this all-too-common financial poison.

This rule states: As your income rises, your spending should fall as a percentage of your earnings.

You might think that earning more is the key to wealth. You're wrong. Earning more without spending less is like trying to fill a leaky bucket. No matter how much water you pour in, it will never be full. It doesn't matter if you're a minimum wage worker or a CEO. The moment your pay check increases, your savings rate should increase even more.

Consider the "Millionaire Next Door" phenomenon. Most millionaires drive used cars, live in modest homes, and spend far less than they earn. They're not misers; they're masters of this rule.

Violating this principle is a one-way ticket to financial stress. That bigger house, fancier car, or designer wardrobe isn't a reward - it's a ball and chain.

The Lifestyle Deflation Doctrine works hand in hand with The Compound Effect (Rule 1). Every dollar not spent is a dollar put to work in the compound interest factory.

This rule isn't about deprivation. It's about intentionality. Choose to spend on what truly matters to you, and ruthlessly cut everything else.

The surest path to financial ruin isn't a market crash or a bad investment. It's lifestyle inflation.

This rule is simple: spend less than you earn. Always. No exceptions.

It sounds obvious, doesn't it? Yet it's astonishingly rare. A 2019 Federal Reserve report found that 39% of Americans couldn't cover a $400 emergency expense. They're violating this rule every day.

But what about the wealthy? Surely they're exempt? Think again. A study of 600 millionaires by authors Thomas J. Stanley and William D. Danko revealed a surprising fact: the average millionaire lives well below their means. They drive used cars, live in modest homes, and avoid luxury brands.

Take Sam Walton, founder of Walmart. Despite being one of the richest men in America, he drove a 1979 Ford F-150 pickup truck. He understood the Rule of Living Below Your Means.

"But I don't want to live like a miser!" you might protest. Good news: you don't have to. This rule isn't about deprivation. It's about intentionality. It's choosing to spend on what truly matters to you and ruthlessly cutting everything else.

Consider the 50/30/20 budget: 50% on needs, 30% on wants, and 20% on savings and debt repayment. This isn't a constraint. It's a framework for freedom.

Many people believe that once they "make it," they can relax this rule. They're wrong. The more you earn, the more important this rule becomes. Just ask Johnny Depp, who reportedly spent $2 million a month and ended up in financial trouble despite earning over $650 million in his career.

The Rule of Living Below Your Means is the foundation of all financial success. Without it, no amount of income, no brilliant investment strategy, no financial windfall can secure your future.

Ignore this rule, and you'll always be one pay check away from financial disaster. Embrace it, and you'll build a fortress of financial security that can weather any storm.

Remember: True financial freedom isn't about affording everything - it's about needing very little.

The Lifestyle Deflation Doctrine sets the stage for The Cushion Commandment (Rule 3) and is a practical application of The Gratification Postponement Principle (Rule 8).

Prediction: By 2060, society will have split into two classes: the "Financially Free" who mastered lifestyle deflation, and the "Wage Slaves" who didn't. Your spending habits today are determining which group you'll belong to.

Rule 3: The Cushion Commandment

Your emergency fund is the difference between a setback and a catastrophe

In 2008, Lehman Brothers, a 158-year-old financial giant, collapsed overnight. Why? They had no cushion to absorb unexpected shocks.

The Cushion Commandment is your personal insurance against becoming the Lehman Brothers of your neighbourhood.

This rule decrees: Maintain 3-6 months of living expenses in easily accessible savings. Always.

You might think you're invincible. Your job is secure, your health is good, and your car runs like a dream. You're wrong. Life has a nasty habit of throwing curveballs when you least expect them.

Whether you're flipping burgers or flipping companies, this rule is non-negotiable. An emergency fund isn't a luxury; it's a necessity.

The road to financial ruin is paved with unforeseen circumstances. Your defense? The emergency fund.

You might think you're invincible. Your job is secure, your health is good, and your car runs like a dream. You're wrong. Life has a nasty habit of throwing curveballs when you least expect them.

Consider the 2020 pandemic. Those with emergency funds weathered the storm. Those without? They're still trying to catch up.

The Cushion Commandment works in tandem with The Protection Paramount Principle (Rule 16). Together, they form an impenetrable shield against life's financial curveballs.

This isn't about paranoia; it's about preparation. Your emergency fund is your financial shock absorber, allowing you to take calculated risks in pursuit of greater wealth.

But what about credit cards? Surely they're a suitable emergency fund? Wrong. Using credit for emergencies is like using gasoline to put out a fire. You're not solving the problem; you're making it worse.

Take Dave Ramsey, personal finance guru. He went from millionaire to bankrupt in his 20s. His comeback strategy? He started with a $1,000 emergency fund. He understood the Rule of Emergency Funds.

"But I can't afford to save!" you might protest. Can you afford not to? An emergency fund isn't a luxury. It's a necessity. It's financial oxygen. Without it, you're one unexpected event away from financial suffocation.

Consider this: A 2019 Federal Reserve study found that 40% of Americans would struggle to cover a $400 emergency expense. They're violating this rule every day, living on a financial tightrope without a safety net.

Many believe that once they have some investments, they don't need an emergency fund. They're dead wrong. Investments are for growing wealth, not for emergencies. Liquidating investments in a crisis is like selling your house because you're hungry.

The Rule of Emergency Funds is your first line of defense against financial chaos. Without it, you're exposed to every financial wind that blows. With it, you have a fortress that can withstand unexpected storms.

Ignore this rule, and you'll always be one emergency away from financial disaster. Embrace it, and you'll sleep soundly knowing you're prepared for whatever life throws your way.

Remember: In finance, as in skydiving, it's not the fall that kills you - it's the sudden stop at the end. Your emergency fund is your parachute.

The Cushion Commandment is a practical application of The Lifestyle Deflation Doctrine (Rule 2) and supports The Multiple Streams Mandate (Rule 9) by providing the security to explore diverse income sources.

Prediction: By 2070, those without robust emergency funds will be legally classified as financially unstable, facing restricted access to credit, housing, and even certain jobs. Your cushion won't just be a safety net - it'll be your ticket to societal participation.

Rule 4: The Diversification Decree

Don't put all your eggs in one basket - or even in one henhouse

In 2001, Enron employees lost their life savings when the company collapsed. In 2000, it was America's seventh-largest company. By 2001, it was worthless. Employees who had their entire 401(k) in Enron stock lost everything. Their crime? Violating The Diversification Decree.

This rule commands: Spread your investments across different asset classes, sectors, and geographies. No exceptions.

You might think you've found the next big thing - the stock that will soar, the crypto that will moon, the real estate market that will never crash. You're wrong. The graveyard of financial ruin is filled with those who bet it all on one horse. It doesn't matter if you're investing $100 or $100 million. Concentration might make you rich, but diversification will keep you rich.

Consider the 2008 financial crisis. Those with diversified portfolios took a hit but recovered. Those all-in on real estate or banking stocks? Many never recovered.

The Diversification Decree works in harmony with The Asset Allocation Axiom (Rule 12). Together, they create a robust, all-weather portfolio that can withstand any economic storm.

This isn't about mindless scattering of assets. It's about strategic allocation. Your diversification should be as unique as your fingerprint, tailored to your goals and risk tolerance.

It sounds obvious, doesn't it? Yet it's astonishingly rare. A 2018 Gallup poll found that 37% of Americans think real estate is the best long-term investment. They're putting all their eggs in one very large, very fragile basket.

But what about Warren Buffett? Didn't he say, "Diversification is protection against ignorance"? Yes, but remember: Buffett's Berkshire Hathaway is itself a diversified portfolio. He understands the Rule of Diversification better than most.

Take Ray Dalio, founder of the world's largest hedge fund. His "All Weather" portfolio is designed to perform in any economic environment. Why? Because he understands that predicting the future is impossible, but preparing for it is essential.

"But diversification limits my gains!" you might protest. True, but it also limits your losses. And in investing, avoiding big losses is more important than making big gains. A 50% loss requires a 100% gain just to break even.

Consider the dot-com bubble of the late 1990s. Those who diversified survived. Those who went all-in on tech stocks?

They're still recovering.

Many believe that as long as they own many stocks, they're diversified. They're wrong. True diversification goes beyond stocks. It includes bonds, real estate, commodities, and even cash. It's not about having many of one thing; it's about having some of many things.

The Rule of Diversification is your insurance against the unpredictable nature of markets and economies. Without it, you're a sitting duck for the next market crash, industry disruption, or economic downturn. With it, you're prepared for whatever the financial future holds.

Ignore this rule, and you're always one market shift away from financial ruin. Embrace it, and you build a portfolio that can weather any storm.

Remember: In investing, as in nature, diversity equals resilience. The ability to survive is often more important than the ability to thrive.

The Diversification Decree complements The Multiple Streams Mandate (Rule 9) by applying the same principle of risk reduction to your investments. It also supports The Protection Paramount Principle (Rule 16) by safeguarding your wealth against sector-specific downturns.

Prediction: By 2060, AI-driven hyper-diversification will make today's notion of diversification look as primitive as bartering. Those who master this rule now will seamlessly adapt to the future of investing, while others scramble to catch up in a world where traditional asset classes have blurred beyond recognition.

Rule 5: The Autopilot Advantage

Remove emotion from the equation and watch your wealth soar

In 2015, a Fidelity study found that their best-performing accounts belonged to investors who had forgotten they had accounts. The Autopilot Advantage at work.

This rule dictates: Automate your financial decisions to bypass human error and emotion.

You might think you have the discipline to save and invest regularly. You're wrong. Human nature is working against you every step of the way. Whether you're a seasoned investor or just starting out, your worst enemy in finance is often yourself. Automation is your shield against your own worst instincts.

Consider Jack Bogle, founder of Vanguard. He revolutionized investing by creating index funds - the ultimate form of financial autopilot. Result? Trillions in wealth created for everyday investors.

The Autopilot Advantage supercharges The Compound Effect (Rule 1) by ensuring consistent, emotion-free investing. It's also a practical application of The Gratification Postponement Principle (Rule 8), automatically diverting funds from immediate wants to long-term needs.

This isn't about abdicating responsibility. It's about designing a system that works even when you're not paying attention. Your financial autopilot is your 24/7 wealth-building employee.

This rule is simple: Automate your savings and investments. Always.

It sounds trivial, doesn't it? Yet it's revolutionary. A study by National Bureau of Economic Research found that automatic enrollment in 401(k) plans increased participation from 37% to 86%. That's the power of automation.

But what about timing the market? Shouldn't you decide when to invest? Wrong. Trying to time the market is a fool's errand. Even professional fund managers fail at it consistently.

Take Jack Bogle, founder of Vanguard. He championed index funds and automatic investing. Why? Because he understood that consistency, not timing, is the key to long-term wealth.

"But I like control!" you might protest. Good news: automation gives you control. It's not about relinquishing decision-making; it's about making the right decision once and letting it work for you repeatedly.

Consider David Bach's "Latte Factor." He showed how automatically saving small amounts daily can lead to significant wealth over time. It's not about the amount; it's about the consistency that automation provides.

Many believe that they need to actively manage their investments to succeed. They're dead wrong. A famous 20-year study by Fidelity found that the best-performing accounts belonged to investors who forgot they had accounts. Why? Because they didn't tinker. Automation kept them invested.

The Rule of Automation is your defense against your own worst financial enemy: yourself. Without it, you're at the mercy of willpower, emotion, and procrastination. With it, you build wealth steadily and surely, regardless of market conditions or personal whims.

Ignore this rule, and you'll always be one impulse purchase away from derailing your financial future. Embrace it, and you'll harness the power of consistency and compound interest.

Remember: In finance, as in aviation, human error is the leading cause of crashes. Your autopilot is your co-pilot, keeping you on course when emotions might lead you astray.

The Autopilot Advantage supports The Knowledge Leverage Law (Rule 6) by freeing up mental bandwidth for continuous financial learning. It's also crucial for implementing The Asset Allocation Axiom (Rule 12), maintaining your ideal portfolio mix through automated rebalancing.

Prediction: By 2075, manual financial management will be viewed as a form of self-harm. Those who resist automation will be treated like addicts, with interventions staged by friends and family to force them into AI-managed financial systems. Start building your autopilot now, or risk becoming a financial Luddite in an automated world.

Rule 6: The Knowledge Leverage Law

Your most valuable asset isn't in your bank account - it's between your ears

In 1997, Amazon was a small online bookstore. By 2023, it was a trillion-dollar company. The secret? Jeff Bezos's insatiable appetite for knowledge and learning.

The Knowledge Leverage Law states: Your financial intelligence determines your financial destiny.

You might think you don't need to understand finance. The "experts" will handle it, right? Wrong. Delegating your financial decisions without understanding them is like handing over the keys to your house to a stranger. It doesn't matter if you're living paycheck to paycheck or sitting on millions. In finance, what you don't know can (and will) hurt you.

Consider Warren Buffett, who spends 80% of his working day reading and thinking. He's not just accumulating information;

he's compounding knowledge.

The Knowledge Leverage Law is the foundation for mastering The Tax Tactician's Triumph (Rule 10) and The Asset Allocation Axiom (Rule 12). It's the key that unlocks every other rule in this book.

This isn't about becoming a financial expert overnight. It's about continuous, lifelong learning. Your financial education is never complete; it's a journey, not a destination.

You might think you don't need to understand finance. The "experts" will handle it, right? Wrong. Delegating your financial decisions without understanding them is like handing over the keys to your house to a stranger.

Consider the 2008 financial crisis. Millions lost their homes because they didn't understand the mortgages they were signing. They violated the Rule of Financial Education.

This rule is simple: Never stop learning about money. Ever.

It sounds obvious, doesn't it? Yet it's shockingly rare. A 2022 TIAA Institute study found that only 34% of Americans could answer basic financial literacy questions correctly. They're financially illiterate in a world that demands financial fluency.

But what about professional advice? Surely that's enough? Wrong. Financial advisors are guides, not guarantors. Without basic knowledge, you can't even tell if the advice you're getting is good.

Take Warren Buffett. He reads 500 pages a day, mostly about finance and business. Why? Because he understands that knowledge compounds just like interest.

"But finance is boring!" you might protest. Is poverty more exciting? Financial education doesn't mean becoming an economist. It means understanding enough to make informed decisions and spot red flags.

Consider Robert Kiyosaki, author of "Rich Dad Poor Dad." He emphasizes financial education over quick-fix solutions. Why? Because he knows that true wealth comes from understanding, not just earning.

Many believe that financial education is only for the rich. They're dead wrong. It's most crucial for those with limited resources. When you can't afford mistakes, you can't afford ignorance.

The Rule of Financial Education is your shield against financial predators and your own ignorance. Without it, you're navigating a financial minefield blindfolded. With it, you have a map and night-vision goggles.

Ignore this rule, and you'll always be at the mercy of those who know more than you. Embrace it, and you'll be equipped to build and protect your wealth in any economic climate.

Remember: In finance, as in chess, the player who sees more moves ahead usually wins. Your financial knowledge is your ability to see those moves.

The Knowledge Leverage Law enhances The Frugal Innovation Formula (Rule 13) by equipping you with the insights needed for creative financial solutions. It's also crucial for implementing The Perpetual Pivot Protocol (Rule 15), as it provides the basis for informed financial adaptations.

Prediction: By 2050, financial literacy will be mandatory, with government-imposed penalties for those who fail to meet minimum standards. Financial ignorance will be treated as a public health crisis, with forced 're-education' for repeat offenders. Start your financial education now, or risk becoming a second-class citizen in a world where financial knowledge is power.

Rule 7: The Debt Destroyer Directive

Slay the debt dragon or be consumed by it

In 2010, Greece's debt crisis brought the country to its knees, forcing harsh austerity measures on its citizens. The Debt Destroyer Directive, ignored on a national scale.

This rule commands: Eliminate toxic debt aggressively and use beneficial debt sparingly.

You might think all debt is created equal. You're wrong. Debt is a tool, and like any tool, it can build or destroy depending on how you use it. Whether you're drowning in credit card bills or contemplating a mortgage, this rule is your lifeline in a sea of potential financial ruin.

Consider Dave Ramsey, who went from millionaire to bankrupt, then rebuilt his wealth by religiously following this principle. His "debt snowball" method has since freed millions from financial bondage.

The Debt Destroyer Directive works hand in hand with The Lifestyle Deflation Doctrine (Rule 2), freeing up resources to tackle debt aggressively. It's essential for fully leveraging The Compound Effect (Rule 1), as debt is often the biggest obstacle to building wealth.

This isn't about avoiding all debt. It's about understanding the difference between destructive debt (credit cards, payday loans) and potentially beneficial debt (mortgages, business loans). Your approach to debt can make or break your financial future.

You might think all debt is created equal. You're wrong. Debt is a tool, and like any tool, it can build or destroy depending on how you use it.

Consider the 2008 housing crisis. Millions took on mortgages they couldn't afford, believing all real estate debt was "good debt." They violated the Rule of Debt Aversion.

This rule is simple: Avoid bad debt like the plague, use good debt sparingly.

It sounds straightforward, doesn't it? Yet it's widely misunderstood. A 2021 Experian report showed the average American carried $92,727 in consumer debt. They're confusing leverage with lifestyle.

But what about "buy now, pay later" schemes? Surely they're harmless? Wrong. They're wolves in sheep's clothing, designed to make you spend money you don't have on things you don't need.

Take Mark Cuban, billionaire entrepreneur. He advises, "Credit cards are the worst investment that you can make." Why? Because he understands the destructive power of high-interest consumer debt.

"But I need debt to build credit!" you might protest. Building credit doesn't mean carrying balances. It means using credit responsibly and paying it off immediately.

Many believe that some debt is unavoidable. They're partially right. But there's a gulf of difference between a mortgage on a reasonably priced home and a loan for a luxury car you can't afford.

The Rule of Debt Aversion is your safeguard against financial bondage. Without it, you're always one purchase away from a debt spiral. With it, you use debt strategically to build wealth, not to finance a lifestyle.

Ignore this rule, and you'll spend your life working for the bank. Embrace it, and you'll make money work for you instead.

Remember: In finance, as in health, prevention is better than cure. Avoiding toxic debt is far easier than trying to dig yourself out later.

The Debt Destroyer Directive supports The Freedom Formula (Rule 20) by removing the shackles of financial obligations. It also reinforces The Brutal Honesty Benchmark (Rule 14), forcing you to confront the true cost of your spending habits.

Prediction: By 2075, personal debt will be monitored like carbon emissions. Individuals will have 'debt quotas,' and exceeding them will result in public shaming and restricted access to services. Debt-free living will be the new symbol of elite status. Start slaying your debt dragon now, or risk becoming a financial pariah in a world where freedom from debt is the new wealth.

Rule 8: The Gratification Postponement Principle

Master your impulses, master your financial future

In the 1960s, psychologist Walter Mischel conducted the famous "marshmallow experiment." Children who could resist eating one marshmallow to get two later were more successful in life. The Gratification Postponement Principle, scientifically proven.

This rule declares: Delay immediate pleasures for greater future rewards. Always.

You might think that enjoying life means spending freely today. You're wrong. True financial freedom comes from mastering the art of waiting. Whether you're tempted by the latest smartphone or a luxury vacation, this rule is your shield against impulsive financial decisions.

Consider Warren Buffett, who still lives in the same house he bought in 1958. He's not depriving himself; he's choosing long-term wealth over short-term indulgences.

The Gratification Postponement Principle is the psychological backbone of The Compound Effect (Rule 1) and The Lifestyle Deflation Doctrine (Rule 2). It's the mental muscle that makes all other financial rules possible.

This isn't about never enjoying life. It's about understanding that true enjoyment comes from freedom, not fleeting pleasures. Your ability to delay gratification is your superpower in building wealth.

Consider the famous Stanford marshmallow experiment. Children who could resist eating one marshmallow to get two later were more successful in life. They intuitively understood the Rule of Delayed Gratification.

This rule is simple: Prioritize tomorrow's wealth over today's wants.

It sounds like common sense, doesn't it? Yet it's astonishingly rare. A 2019 Charles Schwab survey found that 59% of Americans live paycheck to paycheck. They're sacrificing their future on the altar of instant gratification.

But what about "You Only Live Once"? Surely life is meant to be enjoyed now? Wrong. YOLO is financial suicide disguised as life advice. True enjoyment comes from security, not fleeting pleasures.

Take Warren Buffett. He still lives in the same house he bought in 1958 for $31,500. Why? Because he understands that real wealth is about freedom, not flashiness.

"But life is short!" you might protest. Exactly. It's too short to spend it stressed about money. Delayed gratification isn't about never enjoying life; it's about enjoying it sustainably.

Consider millionaire David Bach's "Latte Factor." It's not about the coffee; it's about the compounding effect of small, regular sacrifices. Why? Because he knows that financial freedom is built one small decision at a time.

Many believe that delayed gratification means a life of deprivation. They're dead wrong. It's about prioritizing what truly matters and cutting ruthlessly what doesn't.

The Rule of Delayed Gratification is your ticket to financial freedom. Without it, you're always one impulse buy away from derailing your future. With it, you're consistently building a fortress of financial security.

Ignore this rule, and you'll always be a slave to your wants. Embrace it, and you'll be the master of your financial destiny.

Remember: In finance, as in fitness, the pain of discipline is far less than the pain of regret. Every dollar saved today is freedom bought for tomorrow.

This principle is crucial for implementing The Frugal Innovation Formula (Rule 13), pushing you to find creative alternatives to immediate spending. It also reinforces The Decade Domination Doctrine (Rule 19) by fostering a long-term mindset.

Prediction: By 2090, delayed gratification will be chemically enforced. Those opting into financial success programs will receive regular injections that neurologically reward saving and punish impulsive spending. Instant gratification will be seen as a debilitating mental disorder. Start training your financial willpower now, or risk becoming a slave to your impulses in a world where self-control is the most valued currency.

Rule 9: The Multiple Streams Mandate

Diversify your income or die financially

In 2020, millions lost their jobs overnight due to a global pandemic. Those with multiple income streams survived. Those relying on a single paycheck? They learned the hard way about The Multiple Streams Mandate.

This rule commands: Create and maintain diverse sources of income. No exceptions.

You might think your steady job is all you need. You're wrong. In today's volatile economy, relying on a single income stream is like trying to balance on one leg - it works until it doesn't. Whether you're a janitor or a CEO, relying on a single income source is financial Russian roulette.

Consider Robert Kiyosaki, author of "Rich Dad Poor Dad." He advocates for multiple income streams through investments, businesses, and passive income. Result? Financial resilience in any economic climate.

The Multiple Streams Mandate is a practical application of The Diversification Decree (Rule 4), extending the principle from investments to income sources. It supports The Cushion Commandment (Rule 3) by providing additional financial security.

This isn't about working multiple jobs until you drop. It's about strategically creating income sources that work for you, even when you're not working. Your goal is to make money while you sleep.

Consider Kodak. For decades, it was synonymous with photography. Then digital cameras arrived, and Kodak filed for bankruptcy. They violated the Rule of Income Streams.

This rule is simple: Diversify your income sources. Always.

It sounds obvious, doesn't it? Yet it's remarkably uncommon. A 2019 Bankrate survey found that only 43% of Americans had a side hustle. The rest are putting all their eggs in one fragile basket.

But what about focusing on your career? Surely that's the path to success? Wrong. Even high-paying careers can disappear overnight. Just ask the travel agents replaced by online booking sites.

"But I don't have time for multiple jobs!" you might protest. Good news: multiple income streams doesn't mean multiple jobs. It means creating systems that generate income with or without your active involvement.

Consider Pat Flynn, who went from laid-off architect to multimillionaire through multiple online income streams. Why did he succeed? Because he didn't rely on a single source of income.

Many believe that a high-paying job is the ultimate financial security. They're dead wrong. No job, no matter how high-paying, is truly secure in today's rapidly changing economy.

The Rule of Income Streams is your insurance against economic uncertainty. Without it, you're always one layoff away from financial disaster. With it, you've built a network of financial safety nets.

Ignore this rule, and you'll always be at the mercy of a single employer or client. Embrace it, and you'll have the freedom and security that comes from diverse income sources.

Remember: In nature, a tree with many roots is nearly impossible to topple. In finance, multiple income streams create the same stability.

This rule enhances The Freedom Formula (Rule 20) by reducing dependence on any single income source. It also complements The Frugal Innovation Formula (Rule 13), as creating new income streams often requires creative thinking.

Prediction: By 2050, single-income individuals will be classified as financially disabled. Government programs will forcibly diversify income streams for these 'at-risk' individuals, assigning side gigs and investments to ensure economic stability. Start building your income portfolio now, or risk becoming a ward of the state in a world where financial mono-cropping is seen as a form of self-harm.

Rule 10: The Tax Tactician's Triumph

Master the tax code or be mastered by it

In 2020, it was revealed that Donald Trump, a self-proclaimed billionaire, paid just $750 in federal income taxes in 2016 and 2017. Love him or hate him, he's a master of The Tax Tactician's Triumph.

This rule dictates: Structure your finances to legally minimize your tax burden. Always.

You might think taxes are just a fact of life, unavoidable and uncontrollable. You're wrong. Tax efficiency is the difference between building wealth and treading water financially. Whether you're making minimum wage or millions, ignorance of tax law is bleeding you dry.

Consider General Electric. In 2010, they paid $0 in U.S. taxes on $14.2 billion in profits. How? They understood that the tax code is a game, and they played to win.

The Tax Tactician's Triumph amplifies the impact of The Compound Effect (Rule 1) by ensuring more of your money stays invested. It's a sophisticated application of The Knowledge Leverage Law (Rule 6), turning financial wisdom into tangible savings.

This isn't about tax evasion. It's about tax avoidance - legally minimizing your tax burden. Your goal is to pay every cent you owe, but not a penny more.

This rule is simple: Structure your finances to legally minimize your tax burden. Always.

It sounds straightforward, doesn't it? Yet it's widely overlooked. A 2019 survey by GOBankingRates found that 37% of Americans don't even know their tax bracket. They're handing over more of their hard-earned money than necessary.

But isn't tax avoidance illegal? Wrong. Tax evasion is illegal. Tax avoidance - legally minimizing your tax burden - is not just legal, it's smart financial planning.

Take Warren Buffett. He's famously said he pays a lower tax rate than his secretary. Why? Because he understands how to structure his wealth in a tax-efficient manner.

"But I'm not rich enough to worry about taxes!" you might protest. Wrong again. Tax efficiency matters at every income level. Even small tax savings, invested wisely, can compound into significant wealth over time.

Consider the Roth IRA. It's a powerful tool for tax-free growth, yet many don't utilize it fully. Why? Because they don't understand the long-term tax implications of their financial decisions.

Many believe that tax planning is only for the wealthy. They're dead wrong. It's even more crucial for those with limited resources. When every dollar counts, you can't afford to give away more than necessary.

The Rule of Tax Efficiency is your shield against unnecessary wealth erosion. Without it, you're letting the government take a bigger slice of your financial pie than it needs to. With it, you're maximizing every dollar you earn.

Ignore this rule, and you'll always be paying more than you should. Embrace it, and you'll keep more of your hard-earned money working for you instead of the government.

Remember: In finance, as in chess, the rules are the game. Master the rules of taxation, and you've mastered a key part of the financial game.

This rule supports The Asset Allocation Axiom (Rule 12) by considering tax implications in portfolio construction. It also enhances The Frugal Innovation Formula (Rule 13) by finding creative, legal ways to reduce your tax burden.

Prediction: By 2045, AI tax optimization will be mandatory. Those who overpay taxes will face penalties for 'wasting national resources.' Tax efficiency scores will be public, with low scorers facing social ostracism and restricted financial opportunities. Start optimizing your tax strategy now, or prepare to be labelled a financial liability in a world where tax inefficiency is seen as a form of economic treason.

Rule 11: The Target Acquisition Theory

Aim for nothing, and you'll hit it every time

In 1961, President John F. Kennedy set an audacious goal: put a man on the moon by the end of the decade. Eight years later, Neil Armstrong took his giant leap. The Target Acquisition Theory, applied on a national scale.

This rule asserts: Set specific, measurable financial goals. Or accept financial mediocrity.

You might think vague intentions are enough to secure your financial future. Dead wrong. Without specific, written goals, you're financially adrift in a sea of consumer temptations.

Whether you're saving for a house or aiming for early retirement, vague intentions are the enemy of achievement.

Consider Elon Musk. In 2006, he published Tesla's "Secret Master Plan." Every move since, from the Roadster to the Cybertruck, has aligned with those goals. Result? Tesla's now worth more than the next 9 car companies combined.

The Target Acquisition Theory provides direction for The Compound Effect (Rule 1), ensuring your financial growth is purposeful. It's essential for effectively implementing The Asset Allocation Axiom (Rule 12), as your goals determine your ideal asset mix.

This isn't about rigid, inflexible plans. It's about having a clear destination while remaining adaptable about the route. Your financial goals are your North Star, guiding every decision.

This rule is absolute: Set specific, written financial goals or accept financial mediocrity. No exceptions.

Sounds obvious? Then why do 67% of Americans have no written financial plan, according to a 2019 Charles Schwab study? They're financial ships without rudders, destined for the rocks of debt and regret.

But isn't flexibility better than rigid goals? Nonsense. Flexibility without direction is just aimless wandering. Your goals are your financial North Star.

Take Elon Musk. In 2006, he published Tesla's "Secret Master Plan." Every move since, from the Roadster to the Cybertruck, has aligned with those goals. Result? Tesla's now worth more than the next 9 car companies combined.

"But life is unpredictable!" you might whine. Exactly. That's precisely why you need clear goals. They're your financial compass when life's storms hit.

Consider Olympic athletes. They don't "try their best." They set specific medal goals and structure every aspect of their lives around those goals. Your finances deserve the same Olympic-level focus.

Many believe setting financial goals limits their freedom. They're spectacularly wrong. True freedom comes from financial security, not from drifting through life rudderless.

The Rule of Goal Setting is your roadmap to financial success. Without it, you're just hoping to stumble upon wealth. With it, you're engineering your financial future with precision.

Ignore this rule, and you'll always wonder why financial success eludes you. Embrace it, and you'll join the ranks of those who shape their financial destiny instead of being shaped by it.

Remember: In finance, as in archery, you'll never hit a target you can't see. Clarity of purpose is the precursor to financial success.

This rule enhances The Perpetual Pivot Protocol (Rule 15) by providing clear benchmarks for when and how to adjust your financial strategy. It also reinforces The Brutal Honesty Benchmark (Rule 14), forcing you to confront the gap between your goals and your current reality.

Prediction: By 2060, AI will use predictive modelling to assign "financial destinies" based on current behaviors. Those without clear, quantifiable financial goals will be classified as "economically adrift" and face restricted access to financial services. Start setting and pursuing clear financial targets now, or risk becoming a rudderless ship in a world where every financial decision is scrutinized for its goal alignment.

Rule 12: The Asset Allocation Axiom

Your mix matters more than your picks

In 2008, Yale's endowment fund lost 24.6% during the financial crisis. Harvard's lost 27.3%. The difference? Yale's superior asset allocation, courtesy of David Swensen, their chief investment officer.

This rule declares: Your mix of stocks, bonds, and other assets determines 90% of your returns. Ignore at your peril.

You might think picking winning stocks is the key to wealth. You're not just wrong, you're dangerously deluded. Asset allocation - not stock picking - determines 90% of your investment returns. Whether you're managing $1,000 or $1 billion, picking hot stocks is a fool's errand. Your asset allocation is the real driver of long-term returns.

Consider Ray Dalio's "All Weather" portfolio. It's designed to perform in any economic environment, not by picking winners, but by strategically balancing asset classes.

The Asset Allocation Axiom is a sophisticated application of The Diversification Decree (Rule 4), taking it beyond simple variety to strategic balance. It's closely tied to The Knowledge Leverage Law (Rule 6), requiring continuous learning to optimize your allocation.

This isn't about finding a one-size-fits-all solution. It's about tailoring your asset mix to your goals, risk tolerance, and time horizon. Your asset allocation should be as unique as your fingerprint.

This rule is iron-clad: Your mix of stocks, bonds, and other assets matters more than individual picks. Always.

Sounds boring? Tell that to David Swensen, who grew Yale's endowment from $1 billion to $31 billion primarily through asset allocation. He understood what most investors don't: it's not about hitting home runs, it's about consistently getting on base.

But what about Warren Buffett's concentrated portfolio? Irrelevant. You're not Warren Buffett. For mere mortals, broad asset allocation is the only reliable path to wealth.

Take Target Date Funds. They've grown to over $1.9 trillion in assets by 2021. Why? Because they automatically adjust asset allocation based on your retirement date. It's not sexy, but it works.

"But I want to be aggressive!" you might protest. Fine. Be aggressive with your savings rate, not your allocation. Aggression without allocation is just gambling with a fancy name.

Consider the 60/40 portfolio - 60% stocks, 40% bonds. It's beaten most hedge funds over the past decade. Why? Because asset allocation trumps stock picking every time.

Many believe they can outsmart the market. They're not just wrong, they're the market's lunch. Every day, countless "smart" investors lose to simple, well-allocated portfolios.

The Rule of Asset Allocation is your shield against market volatility and your sword for slaying long-term returns. Without it, you're a leaf in the wind of market forces. With it, you're the captain of your financial ship.

Ignore this rule, and you'll always be chasing the next hot stock. Embrace it, and you'll build wealth with the relentless certainty of compound interest.

Remember: In investing, as in cooking, the recipe matters more than any single ingredient. Master the mix, and you'll feast in bull markets and survive bear markets.

This rule supports The Protection Paramount Principle (Rule 16) by strategically managing investment risk. It also enhances The Perpetual Pivot Protocol (Rule 15), providing a framework for adjusting your portfolio as circumstances change.

Prediction: By 2060, traditional asset classes will blur beyond recognition. Quantum computing will create hyper-personalized asset allocation strategies, rebalancing portfolios millions of times per second. Those who cling to outdated notions of stocks and bonds will be financial dinosaurs, extinct in a world of synthetic, AI-generated asset classes. Start mastering asset allocation now, or risk becoming a relic in the museum of financial history.

Rule 13: The Frugal Innovation Formula

Frugal Innovation

Creativity trumps cash every time

In 1995, a computer programmer named Pierre Omidyar launched AuctionWeb as a side project. His first sale? A broken laser pointer for $14.83. That side project? It became eBay, now worth billions. The Frugal Innovation Formula at its finest.

This rule proclaims: Find creative solutions before opening your wallet. Always.

You might think wealth requires spending big. You're not just wrong, you're financially suicidal. True wealth is built on frugal innovation, not lavish expenditure. Whether you're living paycheck to paycheck or swimming in surplus, throwing money at problems is the hallmark of financial incompetence.

Consider Ingvar Kamprad, founder of IKEA. He turned flat-pack furniture into a $40 billion empire. His secret? Frugal innovation at every turn, from product design to store layout.

The Frugal Innovation Formula amplifies The Lifestyle Deflation Doctrine (Rule 2) by finding creative ways to live well for less. It's a practical application of The Knowledge Leverage Law (Rule 6), turning financial wisdom into ingenious solutions.

This isn't about being cheap. It's about being resourceful. Your ability to innovate frugally is your ticket to financial freedom in a world of mindless consumption.

This rule is unbreakable: Find creative solutions before opening your wallet. No exceptions.

Sounds simplistic? Tell that to Ingvar Kamprad, founder of IKEA. He turned flat-pack furniture into a $40 billion empire. His secret? Frugal innovation at every turn.

But what about "investing in yourself"? Sure, but that doesn't mean throwing money at every problem. It means using your most valuable asset: your brain.

Take Mark Zuckerberg. Facebook's early offices were sparse apartments with mattresses on the floor. Why? Because Zuckerberg knew that innovation, not luxury, builds empires.

"But I need the best tools!" you might whine. Wrong. You need the best ideas. A $2,000 laptop won't make you any more productive than a $500 one.

Consider Warren Buffett. He still lives in the same house he bought in 1958 for $31,500. Why? Because he knows that frugality and creativity are the twin engines of wealth.

Many believe that spending money is the answer to financial

problems. They're not just wrong, they're the reason credit card companies are so profitable.

The Rule of Frugal Innovation is your secret weapon in wealth building. Without it, you're always one paycheck away from financial stress. With it, you're constantly expanding your wealth while others expand their debt.

Ignore this rule, and you'll always be a slave to your spending. Embrace it, and you'll find financial solutions that others can't even imagine.

Remember: In finance, as in nature, necessity is the mother of invention. The most valuable solutions often come from constraints, not excess.

This rule supports The Multiple Streams Mandate (Rule 9) by fostering the creativity needed to develop diverse income sources. It also reinforces The Gratification Postponement Principle (Rule 8), pushing you to find innovative alternatives to immediate spending.

Prediction: By 2080, resource scarcity will make frugal innovation a mandatory life skill. Those unable to creatively maximize limited resources will be classified as "economically inept," facing restricted access to goods and services. Frugal innovators will be the new elite, revered for their ability to create abundance from scarcity. Start flexing your frugal innovation muscles now, or risk becoming a financial dinosaur in a world where creativity is the most valuable currency.

Rule 14: The Brutal Honesty Benchmark

Face your financial truth or live a fiscal lie

In 2001, energy giant Enron filed for bankruptcy. The cause? Years of financial deception, not just to investors, but to themselves. The Brutal Honesty Benchmark, ignored with catastrophic consequences.

This rule demands: Be ruthlessly honest about your financial situation. No exceptions.

You might think a little financial "white lie" to yourself is harmless. You're not just wrong, you're sabotaging your entire financial future. Whether you're drowning in debt or sitting on millions, self-deception is financial suicide.

Consider Ray Dalio, founder of the world's largest hedge fund. His principle of "radical transparency" built Bridgewater Associates into a $140 billion behemoth. Why? Because he knows that financial truth, however painful, is the foundation of financial success.

The Brutal Honesty Benchmark is crucial for effectively implementing The Target Acquisition Theory (Rule 11), ensuring your goals are based on reality, not fantasy. It's the foundation for The Perpetual Pivot Protocol (Rule 15), as honest assessment drives meaningful change.

This isn't about self-flagellation. It's about clear-eyed assessment. Your financial honesty is the bedrock upon which all other financial decisions must be built.

This rule is absolute: Be brutally honest about your financial situation. Always.

Sounds simple? Then why do 65% of Americans have no idea how much they spent last month, according to a 2019 U.S. Bank study? They're living in a financial fantasy world, destined for a rude awakening.

But isn't positive thinking important? Sure, but there's a Grand Canyon of difference between optimism and delusion. Financial honesty is the bridge between the two.

Take Ray Dalio, founder of Bridgewater Associates. His principle of "radical transparency" built the world's largest hedge fund. Why? Because he knows that financial truth, however painful, is the foundation of financial success.

"But I don't want to feel bad about my finances!" you might protest. Tough. Short-term discomfort is the price of long-term financial freedom. Grow up.

Consider Dave Ramsey's cult-like following. Why do millions tune in? Because he forces people to confront their financial reality, no matter how ugly. It's not pleasant, but it's powerful.

Many believe that financial ignorance is bliss. They're not just wrong, they're fiscal flat-earthers in a world of financial physics. Reality doesn't care about your feelings.

The Rule of Financial Honesty is your truth serum for wealth building. Without it, you're building your financial house on a foundation of quicksand. With it, you're constructing a fortress of fiscal reality.

Ignore this rule, and you'll always be running from your financial truth. Embrace it, and you'll face your fiscal facts head-on, turning weaknesses into strengths.

Remember: In finance, as in medicine, accurate diagnosis precedes effective treatment. You can't fix what you won't face.

This rule enhances The Freedom Formula (Rule 20) by aligning your financial reality with your true desires. It also reinforces The Knowledge Leverage Law (Rule 6), as honest self-assessment reveals areas where you need to expand your financial education.

Prediction: By 2040, AI-driven financial analysis will make financial self-deception impossible. Those who master honest financial self-assessment now will thrive. Those who don't will be exposed as financial frauds – to themselves and the world. The future belongs to the financially honest, not the self-deluded. Start your ruthless self-assessment today, or be left naked when the tide of technological transparency comes in.

Rule 15: The Perpetual Pivot Protocol

Adapt or die financially

In 1996, Blockbuster declined to buy Netflix for $50 million. By 2010, Blockbuster filed for bankruptcy while Netflix was worth billions. The Perpetual Pivot Protocol, ignored at catastrophic cost.

This rule insists: Continuously review and adjust your financial strategy. Or become extinct.

You might think that once you've set up a financial plan, you're done. You're not just wrong, you're financially extinct. In the financial jungle, only the adaptable survive. Whether you're just starting out or nearing retirement, financial stagnation is a death sentence in a rapidly evolving world.

Consider Amazon. They started selling books online. Now they're in cloud computing, streaming, and even healthcare. Why? Because Jeff Bezos understands that in finance and business, complacency is death.

The Perpetual Pivot Protocol is essential for maintaining The Asset Allocation Axiom (Rule 12) in a changing world. It's a dynamic application of The Knowledge Leverage Law (Rule 6), turning ongoing learning into adaptive strategies.

This isn't about chasing every new financial fad. It's about thoughtful, deliberate evolution. Your financial strategy should be a living document, not a fossil.

This rule is non-negotiable: Review and adjust your financial strategy regularly. No exceptions.

Sounds tedious? Tell that to Ray Dalio, who built Bridgewater Associates into a $140 billion behemoth through constant reassessment and adaptation. He understands what most ignore: yesterday's winning strategy is tomorrow's losing one.

But isn't long-term thinking important? Absolutely. But there's a galaxy of difference between long-term thinking and financial fossilization. Your strategy should be steadfast, your tactics fluid.

Take Apple. They review their product line constantly, killing even successful products to make way for better ones. Why? Because they know that in finance and business, complacency is death.

"But I don't have time to constantly review my finances!" you might whine. Make time, or make peace with poverty. Your choice.

Consider John Bogle, founder of Vanguard. He championed index funds but continuously refined the approach throughout his career. Why? Because even the best strategies need constant tuning.

Many believe that financial planning is a one-time event. They're not just wrong, they're the financial equivalent of dinosaurs watching the approaching asteroid.

The Rule of Continuous Review is your financial fitness regime. Without it, your wealth strategy grows fat and lazy. With it, you're constantly honing your financial physique, ready for whatever economic weather comes your way.

Ignore this rule, and you'll always be fighting yesterday's financial battles. Embrace it, and you'll be ahead of the curve, surfing the waves of economic change while others drown in outdated strategies.

Remember: In finance, as in biology, it's not the strongest that survive, but the most adaptable. Your ability to pivot is your financial immune system.

This rule supports The Multiple Streams Mandate (Rule 9) by encouraging continuous exploration of new income opportunities. It also enhances The Frugal Innovation Formula (Rule 13), pushing you to find new, creative solutions as circumstances change.

Prediction: By 2045, AI-driven financial advisors will offer real-time strategy adjustments based on global economic shifts. Those who master the art of continuous financial review now will seamlessly integrate with these systems. Those who don't will be as relevant as a flip phone in the age of quantum computing. The future belongs to the financially nimble, not the rigid. Start your continuous review process today, or prepare to be a case study in financial Darwinism.

Rule 16: The Protection

Paramount Principle

Shield your wealth or lose it all

In 2008, Lehman Brothers, a 158-year-old financial giant, collapsed overnight. Their fatal flaw? Inadequate protection against market risks. The Protection Paramount Principle, ignored with global consequences.

This rule mandates: Protect what you can't afford to lose. Always.

You might think insurance is a waste of money. You're not just wrong, you're one accident away from financial oblivion. Whether you're building your first emergency fund or managing a multi-million-dollar portfolio, failure to protect your assets is financial Russian roulette.

Consider Lloyd's of London. They've insured everything from Betty Grable's legs to Keith Richards' fingers. Why? Because they understand that in finance, anything valuable is worth protecting.

The Protection Paramount Principle works in tandem with The Cushion Commandment (Rule 3), creating a comprehensive safety net for your finances. It's a crucial complement to The Diversification Decree (Rule 4), protecting your wealth from both market and personal risks.

This isn't about paranoia. It's about prudence. Your protection strategy is your financial bulletproof vest in a world of economic snipers.

This rule is ironclad: Insure anything whose loss would devastate you financially. No exceptions.

Sounds paranoid? Tell that to Bill Gates, who has his voice insured for $10 million. Extreme? Maybe. But he understands what most don't: true wealth isn't just about accumulation, it's about protection.

But isn't self-insurance better? Sometimes, for minor risks. For major ones, it's like bringing a knife to a gunfight. You're outmatched before you start.

Take Warren Buffett's Berkshire Hathaway. They make billions from insurance. Why? Because Buffett knows that in finance, those who control risk control everything.

"But insurance is expensive!" you might complain. Know what's more expensive? Bankruptcy. Medical bills are the leading cause of U.S. bankruptcies. Still think health insurance is too pricey?

Consider Lloyd's of London. They've insured everything from Betty Grable's legs to Keith Richards' fingers. Why? Because they know that in finance, anything valuable is worth protecting.

Many believe insurance is a luxury. They're not just wrong, they're one unfortunate event away from financial ruin. Insurance isn't a cost, it's an investment in security.

The Rule of Insurance is your financial bulletproof vest. Without it, you're naked in a world of financial snipers. With it, you're protected against life's financial headshots.

Ignore this rule, and you'll always be one accident away from poverty. Embrace it, and you'll have the peace of mind to take calculated risks that build real wealth.

Remember: In finance, as in chess, defense is as important as offense. The best offensive strategy can be undone by a single unprotected vulnerability.

This rule supports The Freedom Formula (Rule 20) by providing the security needed to pursue true financial independence. It also reinforces The Brutal Honesty Benchmark (Rule 14), forcing you to confront and prepare for potential financial threats.

Prediction: By 2050, personalized, AI-driven microinsurance will protect against even the most minute risks. Those who understand the value of comprehensive protection now will thrive in this hyper-insured future. Those who don't will be as vulnerable as a smartphone without a case. The future belongs to the protected, not the exposed. Start your insurance audit today, or prepare to be a cautionary tale in the annals of financial disaster.

Rule 17: The Generosity Growth Gambit

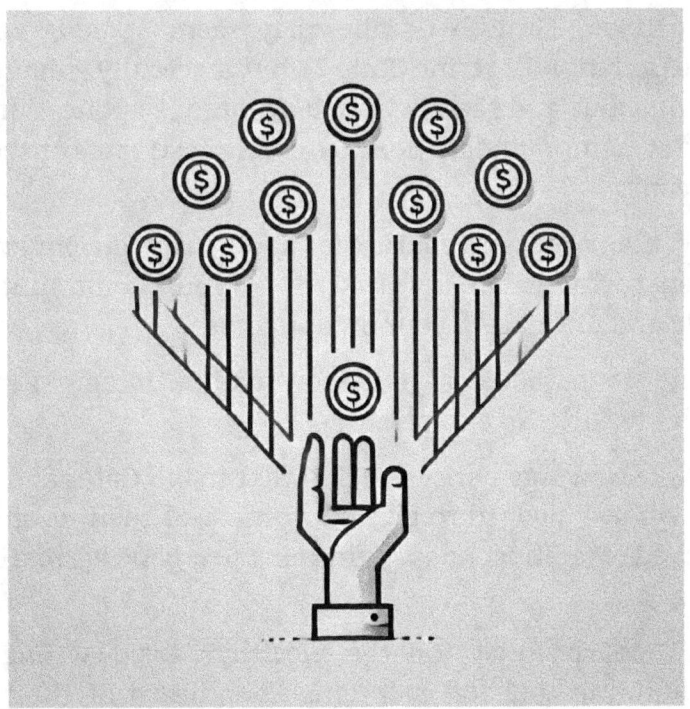

Give more to gain more

In 2010, Bill Gates and Warren Buffett launched The Giving Pledge, committing to donate the majority of their wealth. Their net worths? They've continued to grow. The Generosity Growth Gambit in action.

This rule declares: Strategic generosity multiplies wealth. Counter-intuitive but true.

You might think hoarding every penny is the path to wealth. You're not just wrong, you're sabotaging your own prosperity.

Whether you're living on minimum wage or swimming in millions, calculated giving is a powerful wealth-building tool.

Consider Chuck Feeney, who gave away his entire $8 billion fortune. Result? He's happier than ever and inspired a generation of philanthropists. His secret? Understanding that true wealth isn't just about accumulation.

The Generosity Growth Gambit may seem at odds with The Lifestyle Deflation Doctrine (Rule 2), but it actually enhances it by redefining value and satisfaction. It's a unique application of The Multiple Streams Mandate (Rule 9), creating streams of social and karmic capital.

This isn't about reckless charity. It's about strategic philanthropy. Your generosity is an investment in your community, your network, and ultimately, your own success.

This rule is paradoxical but powerful: Strategic generosity multiplies wealth. No exceptions.

Sounds like New Age nonsense? Tell that to Bill Gates and Warren Buffett, who've pledged to give away most of their wealth. They understand what most miss: giving isn't just good karma, it's good business.

But isn't charity just for the wealthy? Dead wrong. It's a wealth-building tool for everyone. Ever heard of the "helper's high"? It boosts productivity and networking, leading to more opportunities.

Take Patagonia's founder Yvon Chouinard. He just gave away his $3 billion company to fight climate change. Why? Because he knows that in the long run, generosity creates more value than greed.

"But I can't afford to give!" you might protest. You can't afford not to. Start small. Even $5 can change a life – including yours.

Consider the concept of "tithing" in many religions. It's not just spiritual; it's financial wisdom that's stood the test of millennia.

Why? Because givers attract abundance.

Many believe that accumulation is the only path to wealth. They're not just wrong, they're missing out on the multiplier effect of strategic generosity.

The Rule of Giving is your secret weapon in wealth creation. Without it, you're stuck in a scarcity mindset. With it, you're tapping into the abundance of the universe.

Ignore this rule, and you'll always be grasping for more, never satisfied. Embrace it, and you'll find wealth flowing to you in unexpected ways.

Remember: In finance, as in nature, circulation is essential. Money, like water, stagnates when hoarded but creates abundance when it flows.

This rule supports The Freedom Formula (Rule 20) by expanding the definition of wealth beyond mere money. It also reinforces The Knowledge Leverage Law (Rule 6), as strategic giving often leads to new insights and opportunities.

Prediction: By 2055, personal worth will be measured in "Generosity Quotients" rather than net worth. Those failing to meet minimum giving thresholds will face wealth caps and social ostracism. AI will optimize personal giving strategies, making strategic philanthropy a required life skill. Start cultivating your generosity muscles now, or risk becoming a social and financial pariah in a world where giving is the new getting.

Rule 18: The Opportunity Cost Calculus

Every "yes" is a thousand "no's"

In 2007, Microsoft's Steve Ballmer laughed at the iPhone, saying it wouldn't appeal to business customers. By 2017, Apple's market cap had surpassed Microsoft's. The Opportunity Cost Calculus, catastrophically miscalculated.

This rule proclaims: Every financial decision is simultaneously a decision not to do something else. Ignore at your peril.

You might think you're saving money by not investing or skipping that conference. You're not just wrong, you're burning piles of potential wealth. Whether you're deciding on a $5 latte or a $500,000 house, the true cost isn't just the price tag—it's what you're giving up.

Consider Jeff Bezos starting Amazon. He gave up a high-paying Wall Street job. The opportunity cost was huge, but the payoff? He became the world's richest man.

The Opportunity Cost Calculus is crucial for effectively implementing The Gratification Postponement Principle (Rule 8), providing a framework for evaluating trade-offs. It enhances The Frugal Innovation Formula (Rule 13) by pushing you to consider creative alternatives.

This isn't about paralysis by analysis. It's about informed decision-making. Your awareness of opportunity costs is your superpower in a world of infinite choices.

This rule is absolute: Every financial decision you make is simultaneously a decision not to do something else. Always.

Sounds obvious? Then why do 78% of Americans live paycheck to paycheck, according to a 2019 CareerBuilder survey? They're blind to the fortunes they're forfeiting with every frivolous purchase.

But isn't enjoying life important? Sure, but there's a Grand Canyon of difference between enjoyment and indulgence. True enjoyment comes from freedom, not fleeting pleasures.

Take Warren Buffett. He could buy anything, but lives modestly. Why? Because he understands that every dollar spent on luxury is a dollar not compounding in investments.

"But I work hard, I deserve to treat myself!" you might argue. Congratulations, you've just written your ticket to lifelong financial mediocrity.

Consider Jeff Bezos starting Amazon. He gave up a high-paying Wall Street job. The opportunity cost was huge, but the payoff? He became the world's richest man.

Many believe that small expenses don't matter. They're not just wrong, they're compounding their way to poverty one latte at a time.

The Rule of Opportunity Cost is your financial lie detector. Without it, you're living in a fiscal fantasyland. With it, you see the true price of every decision.

Ignore this rule, and you'll always wonder why you can't get ahead financially. Embrace it, and you'll make decisions that compound your wealth exponentially.

Remember: In finance, as in life, you can do anything, but not everything. Every "yes" is implicitly saying "no" to a thousand other options.

This rule reinforces The Decade Domination Doctrine (Rule 19) by encouraging long-term thinking in every financial decision. It also supports The Brutal Honesty Benchmark (Rule 14), forcing you to confront the real implications of your choices.

Prediction: By 2060, AI will calculate and publicly display the lifetime opportunity cost of every purchase in real-time. Those consistently making high opportunity cost choices will be labelled "economic liabilities" and face restricted access to financial services and career opportunities. Social status will be determined by your "Opportunity Optimization Score." Start honing your opportunity cost assessment skills now, or risk becoming a pariah in a world where every financial decision is scrutinized for its long-term impact.

Rule 19: The Decade Domination Doctrine

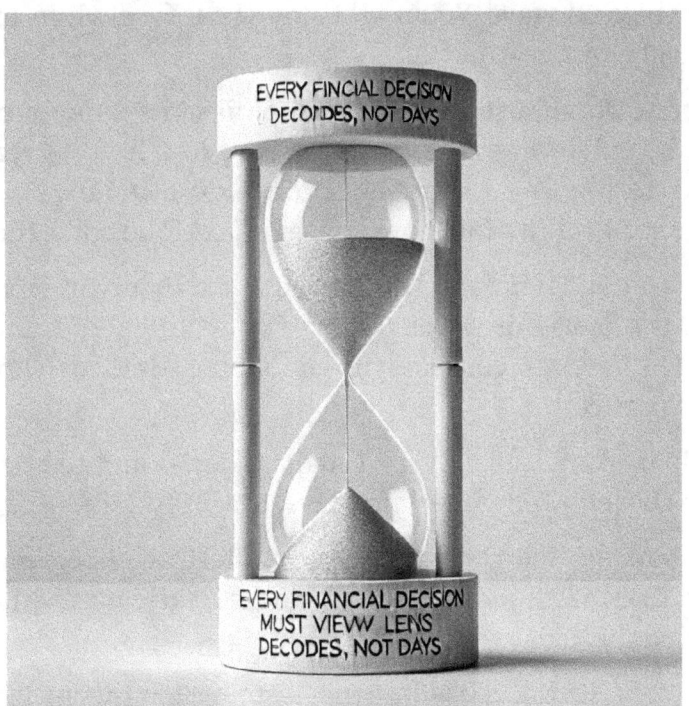

Plan for centuries, not seconds

In 1999, Jack Ma founded Alibaba with a 102-year plan. By 2014, Alibaba's IPO was the largest in history. The Decade Domination Doctrine, executed to perfection.

This rule dictates: Every financial decision must be viewed through the lens of decades, not days. No exceptions.

You might think you're winning by chasing quick gains or instant gratification. You're not just wrong, you're financially suicidal. Whether you're choosing a career or picking an investment, short-term thinking is financial suicide in slow motion.

Consider Warren Buffett, who became one of the world's richest men by holding stocks for decades while others day-traded their way to poverty. His secret? He thinks in decades when others think in days.

Ignoring this rule is like trying to cross the ocean by looking only as far as the next wave. You might stay afloat for a while, but you'll never reach your destination.

The Decade Domination Doctrine amplifies The Compound Effect (Rule 1) by extending the timeframe for growth. It's essential for truly mastering The Asset Allocation Axiom (Rule 12), as long-term thinking allows for more strategic portfolio construction.

This isn't about ignoring the present. It's about understanding how today's decisions shape tomorrow's realities. Your long-term perspective is your compass in the stormy seas of short-term market fluctuations.

This rule is immutable: Every financial decision must be viewed through the lens of decades, not days. No exceptions.

Sounds boring? Tell that to Warren Buffett, who became one of the world's richest men by holding stocks for decades while others day-traded their way to poverty.

But isn't the world changing too fast for long-term planning? Nonsense. The more volatile the world, the more crucial long-term thinking becomes. It's your anchor in the storm of change.

Take Japan's Millennium Corporation. They have a 1,000-year business plan. Extreme? Maybe. But they understand what most miss: true wealth is built across generations, not quarters.

"But I need results now!" you might whine. Congratulations, you've just volunteered to be the plankton in the financial food chain.

Consider Amazon. For years, Wall Street criticized Bezos for not turning a profit. He focused on long-term growth instead. Result? Amazon became a trillion-dollar company.

Many believe that long-term thinking means sacrificing the present. They're not just wrong, they're missing the point entirely. Long-term thinking enhances the present by removing short-term anxieties.

The Rule of Long-Term Thinking is your financial telescope. Without it, you're stumbling around in the dark of immediate gratification. With it, you're navigating by the stars of future prosperity.

Ignore this rule, and you'll always be a slave to financial short-sightedness. Embrace it, and you'll build a legacy while others scramble for scraps.

Remember: In finance, as in chess, grandmasters think several moves ahead. The further ahead you plan, the more likely you are to win the game.

This rule enhances The Target Acquisition Theory (Rule 11) by encouraging the setting of ambitious, long-term financial goals. It also reinforces The Perpetual Pivot Protocol (Rule 15), providing a stable framework within which to make necessary adjustments.

Prediction: By 2070, financial decisions will be evaluated on a multi-generational timeline. Those unable to demonstrate long-term thinking will be classified as "temporally impaired," facing restricted access to loans, investments, and even certain jobs. AI-driven "Timeline Impact Scores" will measure the long-term consequences of every financial choice. Start cultivating your long-term thinking now, or risk becoming a financial fossil in a world where century-long planning is the norm.

Rule 20: The Freedom Formula

Money is a tool, not a goal

In 2015, Patrick Pichette, CFO of Google, quit his high-powered job to travel the world. His reason? "Life is too short." The Freedom Formula, perfectly executed.

This rule declares: True wealth is measured in freedom, not figures. Always.

You might think accumulating wealth is the ultimate goal. You're not just wrong, you're setting yourself up for a life of golden handcuffs. Whether you're earning minimum wage or millions, if you're not building freedom, you're missing the point of money.

Consider Mr. Money Mustache, who retired at 30 not by earning a fortune, but by redefining wealth. His secret? Understanding that financial independence is about needing little, not having much.

The Freedom Formula is the ultimate culmination of The Lifestyle Deflation Doctrine (Rule 2) and The Gratification Postponement Principle (Rule 8), redefining success in terms of freedom rather than consumption. It's supported by The Multiple Streams Mandate (Rule 9), which provides the diversified income needed for true independence.

This isn't about never working again. It's about having the power to choose your work. Your financial freedom is the ability to say "no" to what you don't want and "yes" to what you do.

This rule is supreme: Money is a means to an end, not the end itself. Always.

Sounds philosophical? Tell that to Bill Gates, who's giving away most of his fortune. He understands what most miss: true wealth is measured in freedom, not figures.

But isn't having more money always better? Dead wrong. Beyond a certain point, more money doesn't buy more happiness. It buys more problems.

Take Warren Buffett. He still lives in the same house he bought in 1958. Why? Because he knows that financial independence isn't about having everything, it's about needing very little.

"But I want to be rich!" you might protest. Fine. But ask yourself why. If your answer isn't "to have more freedom," you're on a fool's errand.

Consider the FIRE movement (Financial Independence, Retire Early). Its followers aren't after millions; they're after freedom. They've grasped what most haven't: financial independence is about controlling your time, not your wallet.

Many believe that more money solves all problems. They're not just wrong, they're perpetuating the hamster wheel of endless accumulation.

The Rule of Financial Independence is your true north in the financial wilderness. Without it, you're just a well-paid slave. With it, you're the master of your financial destiny.

Ignore this rule, and you'll always be chasing the next dollar, never satisfied. Embrace it, and you'll find contentment while building real, meaningful wealth.

Remember: In finance, as in life, the quality of your existence is determined by the quality of your choices, not the quantity in your bank account.

This rule gives deeper purpose to The Compound Effect (Rule 1), directing wealth accumulation towards genuine life satisfaction. It also reinforces The Brutal Honesty Benchmark (Rule 14), forcing you to confront what truly matters in your life.

Prediction: By 2080, society will have split into two distinct classes: the "Financially Free" and the "Wage Slaves." The latter, despite their vast resources, will be viewed as modern-day serfs, trapped by their own abundance. True respect will be reserved for those who've mastered the art of minimalism and time affluence, regardless of their bank balance. Start redefining your relationship with money now, or risk becoming a cautionary tale in a world where freedom, not finance, is the true measure of success.

Epilogue

The Financial Symphony

You've now learned the 20 Unbreakable Rules of Personal Finance. But knowing them isn't enough. True financial mastery comes from understanding how these rules work in concert.

Think of these rules as instruments in a grand financial orchestra. The Compound Effect is your steady drumbeat, setting the rhythm of your wealth-building journey. The Lifestyle Deflation Doctrine and the Gratification Postponement Principle form the bass line, providing a solid foundation. The Diversification Decree and Asset Allocation Axiom create harmony, while the Frugal Innovation Formula and the Multiple Streams Mandate add creative flourishes.

The Knowledge Leverage Law is your conductor, ensuring all elements work together seamlessly. And the Freedom Formula? That's the beautiful melody that emerges when all instruments play in perfect sync.

But remember, you are both the composer and the performer of this financial symphony. It's up to you to practice each instrument, to understand how they complement each other, and to create a masterpiece that resonates with your unique life goals.

The future belongs to those who can orchestrate these rules skillfully. Will you be a maestro of your financial destiny, or a mere spectator in the audience of life?

The choice is yours. The baton is in your hand. Now, let the music of your financial freedom begin.

Appendix

Appendix: Key Financial Calculations

1. Compound Interest Formula
2. Rule of 72
3. Emergency Fund Calculation
4. Debt-to-Income Ratio
5. Asset Allocation Percentages
6. Retirement Savings Goal Calculation

Glossary of Terms

1. Asset Allocation: The process of dividing investments among different asset categories like stocks, bonds, and cash.
2. Compound Interest: Interest calculated on the initial principal and the accumulated interest from previous periods.
3. Diversification: Spreading investments across various financial instruments to minimize risk.
4. Emergency Fund: A savings account set aside for unexpected expenses or financial emergencies.
5. Financial Independence: The state of having sufficient wealth to live without having to work actively for basic necessities.
6. Frugal Innovation: The process of reducing the complexity and cost of a good while maintaining or improving its key benefits.
7. Lifestyle Inflation: The tendency to increase spending when income goes up.

8. Opportunity Cost: The loss of potential gain from other alternatives when one alternative is chosen.

9. Passive Income: Income that requires minimal labor to earn and maintain.

10. Risk Tolerance: The degree of variability in investment returns that an investor is willing to withstand.

References

Bogle, J. C. (2007). The Little Book of Common Sense Investing. John Wiley & Sons.

Buffett, M., & Clark, D. (2008). Buffettology: The Previously Unexplained Techniques That Have Made Warren Buffett The World's Most Famous Investor. Simon and Schuster.

Dalio, R. (2017). Principles: Life and Work. Simon and Schuster.

Kiyosaki, R. T. (2017). Rich Dad Poor Dad. Plata Publishing, LLC.

Graham, B. (2006). The Intelligent Investor (Revised Edition). Harper Business.

Ramsey, D. (2013). The Total Money Makeover: A Proven Plan for Financial Fitness. Thomas Nelson.

Robbins, T. (2014). Money: Master the Game: 7 Simple Steps to Financial Freedom. Simon & Schuster.

Sethi, R. (2009). I Will Teach You to Be Rich. Workman Publishing.

Stanley, T. J., & Danko, W. D. (1996). The Millionaire Next Door: The Surprising Secrets of America's Wealthy. Longstreet Press.

Thaler, R. H., & Sunstein, C. R. (2009). Nudge: Improving Decisions About Health, Wealth, and Happiness. Penguin Books.

Vanguard Group. (2021). How America Saves 2021. Vanguard Research.

Federal Reserve. (2020). Report on the Economic Well-Being of U.S. Households in 2019.

Benartzi, S., & Thaler, R. H. (2007). Heuristics and Biases in Retirement Savings Behavior. Journal of Economic Perspectives, 21(3), 81-104.

Malkiel, B. G. (2019). A Random Walk Down Wall Street: The Time-Tested Strategy for Successful Investing (12th ed.). W. W. Norton

& Company.

Zweig, J. (2007). Your Money and Your Brain: How the New Science of Neuroeconomics Can Help Make You Rich. Simon & Schuster.

Ries, A., & Trout, J. (1993). The 22 Immutable Laws of Marketing: Violate Them at Your Own Risk! HarperBusiness.

Bogle, J. C. (2007). The Little Book of Common Sense Investing: The Only Way to Guarantee Your Fair Share of Stock Market Returns. John Wiley & Sons.

Vanguard Group. (2021). Principles for Investing Success. Retrieved from https://personal.vanguard.com/pdf/ISGPRINC.pdf

About the Book

"The 20 Unbreakable Rules of Personal Finance" is not just another financial advice book. It's a paradigm-shifting manifesto designed to revolutionize your relationship with money.

Drawing inspiration from the acclaimed style of "The 22 Immutable Laws of Marketing," this book distills complex financial wisdom into 20 clear, actionable rules. Each rule is presented with stark clarity, backed by real-world examples, and concluded with a bold prediction of how violating it will impact your future in our rapidly changing world.

From the power of compound interest to the necessity of brutal financial honesty, from the surprising growth that comes from strategic generosity to the true meaning of financial freedom - these rules cover the entire spectrum of personal finance.

This book challenges conventional wisdom, provokes thought, and demands action. It's not for the faint of heart or those seeking get-rich-quick schemes. Instead, it's for individuals ready to take control of their financial destiny, armed with timeless principles that work for everyone, regardless of income level or financial status.

Whether you're just starting your financial journey or looking to refine your wealth-building strategy, "The 20 Unbreakable Rules of Personal Finance" provides the framework for lasting financial success in an ever-changing economic landscape.

Remember: These aren't just rules; they're the keys to your financial freedom. Use them wisely.

The 20 Unbreakable Rules of Personal Finance

Master Your Money, Master Your Life: The Ultimate Guide to Financial Freedom

www.ingramcontent.com/pod-product-compliance
Lightning Source LLC
Chambersburg PA
CBHW071954210526
45479CB00003B/934